Camper
Chronicles

by Rae Allen

Keep Living The Dream!

⋙ RAE ⟶

3/1/22

Library of Congress #:

Camper Chronicles / Rae Allen

ISBN: ###-#-###-#####-# (Hardcover)
ISBN: 979-8-410-11206-2 (Paperback)
ISBN: ###-#-###-#####-# (Kindle E-book)

All photos used in this book are in the public domain.
Hey! Don't forget to read the "Foreword" and the "Introduction" before you start in on the rest of this book. Just sayin'... (It's not "Forward" by the way. That's altogether different and just a word often yelled at marching bands by their Drum Majors.)

You are invited to visit the author's Facebook page at
www.facebook.com/dottie.allen.1238

Foreword

I worked for thirty odd years in a number of "8 to 5" jobs, before retiring in 2007. I wrote my first book, entitled "An American Holocaust: The Story of Lataine's Ring", in 2010. It became a best-seller. Twenty-one years later (to my credit), I have written a total of twelve books, all of which have been published worldwide and are being sold at Amazon and Barnes & Noble. The extra income they have generated is very much appreciated, thanks to my loyal readers. Even though I am still able to "make ends meet" with my retirement and Social Security income alone, it has become much more challenging recently, since the onset of the world-wide Covid-19 pandemic. I'm quite certain that many of you can identify with the unfortunate financial uncertainties that have arisen of late, particularly for those of us who are primarily on a fixed income. Personally, I don't know any wealthy self-published authors. I'm sure there are plenty, but I have never written anything to make money. I write because I love it! My books are like my children. They are my creations, and mine alone. I will keep giving birth to such tomes, until the Good Lord decides otherwise.

Roughly three months ago, my sister-in-law told me that one of her friends was ready to edit and publish her first book from the notes she had written during a period of time in her life that was transitional for both her and her husband. They had sold their suburban house of twenty-eight years and had begun building a new house out of town in the idyllic countryside, where they had purchased several acres of undeveloped land. They lived in their camper while their new house was being built. She was unsure of how to begin the "book-making" process and didn't have internet service at her new location. My sister-in-law asked me if I would simply discuss it with her and help her get started. I said sure.

That was just before the Christmas holiday season last year, so all of us were somewhat stretched for time and had precious little extra to devote toward creating a manuscript essentially from scratch. Nevertheless, we had a few discussions, and Dottie "Rae" promised to compile her notes into one document after the holidays.

She contacted me in early January and provided me with her notes, which she had typed and organized by date into a single document. After only a minimal degree of organizing and editing, that document has now been published and sits before you. If you are at all like me, you will absolutely love it. You will laugh out loud... repeatedly! And you will be constantly drawn into a lifestyle that has become commonplace in today's America, yet still remains foreign to most Americans -- life in a tiny camper in the middle of nowhere, instead of living in a house or an apartment complex.

The serendipitous nature of my new friendship with Dottie "Rae" and her chronicles is worth mentioning, as I recount its development into becoming a profound literary work of art, which I am confident you will find it to be. Before I actually read through her compiled manuscript, I purchased my brother's camper, in order to have a place to live while my daughter's house is being renovated. We have an equal interest in the property, but a number of things there need to be changed in order to accommodate the both of us. The renovations will require me moving to her present location in Texas, while the work is being done. I plan to move next month and become a temporary camper dweller myself. I have never lived in a camper, but I have lived in a few small mobile homes in past years. I thought I knew what to expect, but when I finally read through Dottie Rae's book, it was an eye-opener! I can't tell you why without being a spoiler, but you will soon find out.

This book is life as you find it, in all its raw emotion, humor, and grit... as told by someone who has indeed lived the camper life. The <u>Camper Chronicles</u> will take you there, and like Dottie "Rae", you will never be the same. You will be better. When you come to the end of this book, hopefully you will have developed a grace toward others that you probably never knew you needed. Being kind is a process, not a given. Like the author of this book, you too can learn to be a happy camper, regardless of where you may find yourself. Get plenty of rest before you dive into the following pages. You won't want to stop reading, until you reach the final page. --Kerry L. Barger / author, editor, publisher, poet, digital artist, and a camper-in-the-making.

Digitally signed on January 28, 2022 in Oklahoma.

Contents

Camper Chronicles

Introduction

chron.i.cle

noun

plural noun: chronicles

a factual account of important or historical events in the order of their occurrence.

In order to be "in order of occurrence", we have to start with the selling of the home we lived in for twenty-eight years, the home we raised three kids in and where we planned to finish out our years. Moving was never in our retirement vision, and yet here we are.

Once the decision was made, things moved so quickly that it was difficult to keep pace. We put the house up for sale, and it sold in four weeks. We weren't expecting it to sell so quickly and hadn't even begun to pack. Did I mention that we lived there for twenty-eight years? We have a LOT of "stuff"! To say it was overwhelming doesn't even begin to describe the panic attacks I experienced on a daily basis. You also need to understand that all of that "stuff" had to go in the barn. Not only were we not planning on the house selling so quickly, but we hadn't even started building our new house. Thirty-six years of life went into the barn.

Since everything was going in the barn, there needed to be some order to it. Only the things placed in front would be accessible and everything needed to be clearly marked. I needed to decide what I could do without, what I would need to be able to get to quickly, and what bare necessities that I needed in the camper. Extreme organization was required, and there was only thirty days to do it. Anxiety and panic reigned supreme. Fortunately, I am an expert at living in chaos. (I'm not called the Queen of Chaos for nothing.) I knew I could do it. I also knew I would be impossible to live with. But we had reached a point of no return, and it had to be done.

It's all a blur now. I'm not sure how, but we got all our stuff organized, packed and loaded. AND... the marriage remains intact! I'm sure this is a good omen. What can go wrong now?

We are building a house on ten acres of unimproved land in a rural area. We had to build our own road to get to the building site. We just finished building the barn. The electric and water were put in yesterday.

In addition to LIVING in a camper, we will also be living on a building site.

LIVE, not camp. Not vacation... LIVE.

The husband and I are campers. We own a camper. We are experienced. We have done a lot of camping. We have never LIVED in a camper, but how different can it be? Camping is fun, right? Everybody loves to camp. It's a vacation! Woo Hoo! Living the dream! And after all, how long can it take to build a house? Don't we see whole neighborhoods go up overnight? It won't be that big of a deal.......

We loaded the last of it on trailers this morning, took everything to the barn, went to the closing on the sale of our house of twenty-eight years, then came to our new home, our camper!

And thus begins the "CAMPER CHRONICLES"...

Week 1

June 25 / Day 1

We have water. We do NOT have septic.

There is a porta potty here for the construction workers. I've had occasion to use it while we are out here checking on progress and putting things in the barn. Our builder so graciously said we were welcome to use it too. After all...we will be doing our own cleanup of the construction site, so we are part of the construction crew. (Insert eye roll here)

I'd like to say... Porta potties are gross! Eeeewwww! And the ones on construction sites are beyond gross. I can't say gross enough!

I'm not crazy about having to use a porta potty, but I certainly will NOT use the same one as the construction crew. Before you judge me, just know: I am married to an outdoorsman. I hunt. I fish. I pee outside when necessary. I am not prissy. So if I say it's gross, you can believe me.

We have ordered our very own, personal, private porta potty. It will be here Monday. I can't wait!

How sad that my life consists of being excited to get a

porta potty.

June 26 / Day 2

Camping

Where do you sit when you're camping? Outside. So our lawn chairs are outside, just as if we were camping. There's not a lot of seating options inside, which is why people sit outside. The camper is parked under a tree, and the chairs and a wicker table are behind the camper. It's a nice, shady, pleasant spot. It's mostly hard-packed dirt. The builder had the guy doing the dirt work smooth out a pad for us. There are a few blades of grass, which is why after sitting for several minutes looking at the grass next to my shoe, I was GREATLY surprised to see it move! Grass snakes are called grass snakes, because...they look like grass!!!

Mercy! This girl is of the persuasion that there is no good snake. Don't like 'em. Don't want to be around 'em. NO. NO. NO. NO. I screamed a little, did a little jig, and got out of the way, unwittingly holding tightly to my phone. I took a picture of it. That sucker slithered right up into the chair I was sitting in! As if I had inconvenienced it! And it stayed there for quite awhile.

This is not a good omen. This is the second day. What have I gotten myself into?!?!

June 30 / Day 5

Observation: Having less space and less stuff means some things take a longer time, and some things take a shorter time.

Never the same amount of time as before.

I have yet to figure out the time continuum.

Week 2

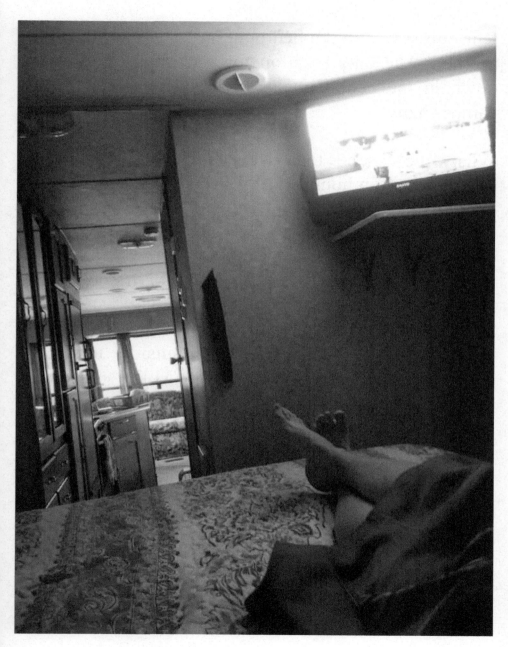

July 2 / Day 7

Our only TV is in the bedroom on a shelf at the foot of the bed. The only position for watching TV is laying down in the bed. Because of this, there are a lot of camper naps.

What's the weather today? Let me watch the news and see ...zzzz......an hour later.....What's the weather today?

Also......remember we have no septic (and no house), so even though I have a washer I have no way to use it. I have to drag laundry to any relative or friend's house kind enough to let me do laundry. It's day 7 and this is already tiresome. We have no place for a hamper, so the dirty clothes go in a basket outside, under the camper. Therefore, someone (Yeah, I'M the someone...) must stay on top of the laundry. No slacking is allowed here.

While at my sister's doing said laundry, my young niece tells me that sometimes she gets up during the night to get a snack. She says she's not supposed to be up, so she just gets a sneaky snack. That is my new favorite thing! "Sneaky Snack!"

Camper naps and sneaky snacks! This camper life may

not be so bad after all.

July 7

Some interesting camper facts:

EVERYTHING in a camper squeaks. The couch, the floors, the cabinets, the table, the seats at the table, the bed, the toilet...yep! Everything.

I tested it. You don't think about it when you're camping. Camping is about fun. You're not inside a lot, and when you are, you're not thinking about noise. But when it's where you live, and you're awake in the night trying to be quiet, that's when you notice everything squeaks.

Campers have a camper smell. You don't think about it when you're camping, because camping is all about having fun. You do know it's there, because when you are getting your camper ready to take on a camping trip you notice it and try to get rid of it. But then you get to camp and don't think of it again. However, if you are living your regular everyday life and dressing for that everyday life... like going to work, or school, or church... and your clothes smell like camper, you notice.

As mentioned before, there is no place inside a camper

for a clothes hamper. I can't figure this one out. There's a closet for clean clothes but what are you supposed to do with the dirty ones? Also mentioned before, I put one outside under the camper. It's the best solution I could come up with, and when we are camping it works great. Keeps the fish smell outside when we are fishing.

Now, what you want to remember is, the best time to check said hamper for snakes that might have crawled in, is BEFORE you get to your sister's house to do laundry. Especially if you want to be welcomed back to do more laundry. If you're going to be depending on her generosity for the foreseeable future, you do want to be welcomed back. This also goes for bugs, spiders, and toads, none of which are welcome in her laundry room.

Them's the facts folks!

July 8

All y'all goin' to the gym, walkin', doin' yoga.......? Pppfffftttt! I just made up the bed and got a full body workout. Have you ever made up the bed in a camper? If you have, high five my friend! If you haven't, you have no idea. There is absolutely NO way to make up a camper bed without doing a full set of calisthenics, a yoga routine, and a good 10 minutes of cardio. But for the most intense workout, change the sheets.

When you're camping, you may or may not even make the bed. You probably won't do it every day, but if the camper is your home you're gonna want to make the bed and change the sheets on a regular basis.

These are just a few things that need to be taken into consideration before becoming "Camper People".

Week 3

July 11

Some of our friends think living in the camper is going to be a strain on our marriage. Well, we've been married 36 years. We've been through quite a bit, and we didn't come this far to be beaten by camper life. But I'm not gonna lie, it's different. It's challenging. I would NOT recommend it, unless you've been married long enough to know how to deal with some serious difficulties. I mean serious like... you have no choice but to work through the difficulties. Because here's the biggest problem... a camper is ONE ROOM. Neither of you is going to the bedroom and slammin' the door. You're right there with each other, and there's no where to go. You better have some resolution skills, or you're gonna be in trouble. There's not a lot of space to be hangin' out all mad at each other.

You can walk around outside, but eventually it will get dark. Then you have to decide if its more important to be mad or take your chances with the snakes. Its best to just work it out. Trust me, no one wants to be stepping on snakes in the dark. You really don't want that.

July 12

The clothes hamper? Again with the hamper... Ugh!

It's summer. But sometimes it rains in the summertime. Being a seasoned camper, I know to push the basket way up under the camper when it rains. But if you're not on a campground and are instead on ten acres when an Oklahoma storm hits...pushing it under won't make a bit of difference.

Nothing says "Hi! New neighbor!" like having your granny panties scattered all over tarnation. "Good Morning, Mr. Marshall! Just gathering my unmentionables off your fence. Have a nice day!"

If you're gonna live in a camper, remember to bring the laundry inside if it rains.

Since we are airing our dirty laundry (literally), let's talk poo.

The porta potty service said they could service our camper! Woo Hoo! At twice the cost of servicing a porta potty. How in the world does that make any sense?! And no thank you. Just bring me a porta potty.

How much does poo cost? Glad you asked! $90 a month! (I KNOW!!) Who knew poo would cost so much?

Don't misunderstand, I am VERY pleased with our porta potty. I'm very happy to have it. And it's clean! The man who services it goes out of his way to make it as nice as possible. (I'm pretty sure he thinks I'm not quite right. I doubt he has any other customers who are as excited to see him as I am. I like my bathroom clean.) He even sprays some kind of deodorizer in there. There's a little mirror in there. We even have a "Private Use" sign on it to keep the construction crew out of it.

But I just thought you might be interested in the price of poo, in case you ever need to live in a camper and don't have septic. Now you know.

July 13

Is it still week 2?

When you live on a building site you never know who will be there when you open your door. I QUICKLY learned to always be dressed! I had roofers yesterday with no shirts. That was (ahem) interesting. Roofers were here again today, but after a trip to the "facilities", no one was here.

I just got home from the grocery store, and when I went to the car to bring in the last of the groceries, workers were here.

It's a surprise EVERY time!

July 15 / Day 20

Trust your instincts. For the most part you will always be right. If your instincts say it's a bad idea to go out for Mexican for dinner (because your facilities are an outhouse), go with your instincts. Otherwise you will be forced to make decisions you never thought you would be forced to make, especially if your almost perfect husband can sleep through anything (i.e., storms, tornado's, tornado sirens, earthquakes, any natural disaster, crying babies, puking babies, or a menopausal wife that tosses and turns constantly). If this is your husband, he is not going to magically appear by your side, ask what's wrong, and then offer to escort you to the outhouse.

Now you should know... you don't place your outhouse close to where you live. Mine is pretty nice, but they don't smell like roses. You don't want that smell in your house, not even a camper house.

It's dark. We have snakes, and as Charlie Pride said, "Snakes Crawl at Night". We have other wild animals at night too, and as evidenced by the special "presents" the neighbors dogs leave. (Poop! They leave poop!) They come into our yard at night.

Do I wake the husband? Experience has taught me that the chances of getting him awake are slim. The chances of getting him awake AND coherent are non-existent.

Do I suck it up, be a big girl, and handle my business?

That does seem the only option.

I need a flashlight and shoes.

What about protection? Probably a good idea.

But, the husband who will sleep through anything will be wide awake and very alert in seconds, if I load the gun. I've already made the "be a big girl" decision. No turning back now.

I could load it outside.

The problem with that is: IF he woke up and couldn't find me, then went outside to look for me, and I have a loaded firearm and hear something prowling around outside... AND I'm already a little scared..........

Did I mention that not following your instincts will result in making decisions you never ever thought you would have to make? Decisions you might need to make in a hurry? Decisions you might have to make in a hurry when you are really not at your best?

We survived the night. We are both well. I decided on just the flashlight, hoping the light would deter any danger.

It's Day 20. Y'all pray for our builder. We need a house ASAP!

July 17

Three weeks have passed today / Happy Anniversary!

Let's talk optics. As mentioned previously, the placing of the outhouse is very important. Not too close to where you live (because...eeewwwww!), but close enough to be convenient. Should be easy enough. Except, if you remember, we live on the construction site. So we have construction workers ALL THE TIME.

The whole south side of the house is windows (or...where the windows go), so that's where they stand to get relief from the 100 degree temperatures. There is someone standing there at all times. The camper is beside the construction site of our new house, and someone decided the best place for the outhouse is on the south side of the camper. The result is, the construction crew always has a "view" of our "private" porta potty.

Most likely they could care less about anything but finishing their job, but every time they take a break, they see what's going on at the outhouse.

I'm no spring chicken, and I am not supermodel

material. But I am the only woman here. So yeah, they're gonna at least notice.

And that brings us back to decisions you never thought you would have to make, when in a hurry.

Do I wear my pajama's to go to the porta potty? No? Then I will have to dress for the occasion. What to wear? Can I wear what I had on yesterday? Normally not an issue, but again, I'm the only woman here. Will they remember? Will they care? Do I care if they care? (Some of you know you would be thinking the same thing.) Well, I definitely don't want to wear my good clothes. What to do?

Also...how much coffee do I REALLY need? How many times can I go out before they start placing bets?

Over think it (Yeah, that's my superpower!), and it won't take long before you have a different kind of issue to deal with.

Optics. We should have put the outhouse somewhere else.

I hope at least one of you builds a house and learns from my experience.

Week 4

July 18

The dog. Yeah we have a dog. I should at least mention him. He barks at the construction guys... all the time.

He lives in the camper too. He's an inside dog. He doesn't like the camper, but he tolerates it. He's unsure about all the construction activity. He can't figure out what his role is. He wants to defend his territory from all the strangers, but he loves people. So he's confused.

IF you didn't know... the camper is basically just a tin box. It's summer in Oklahoma. I can't take the dog when I leave, because I can't leave him in the car. I can't leave him outside, because I don't trust the neighbors dogs. I'm afraid to leave him in the camper, because its a construction site and anything could happen to cause the electric to go out and a tin box will heat up pretty quick. This means that any time I leave, I have to make some kind of provision for the dog. Everyone loves this dog, unless you need a dog sitter. Then.........everyone's busy.

I never thought that at fifty-four years of age my whole life would be reduced down to laundry, a dog, and an outhouse. I am livin' the dream folks!

July 19

All of this is taking place during a world-wide pandemic.

That's why we didn't think our house would sell so quickly, and why we were unprepared. That's why we don't have the options we would otherwise have. That's why we have trouble getting work crews. That's why we have such long waits for materials. That's why we sit in the camper for days and see no progress. That's why, if we let ourselves, we could get really discouraged.

But...no need for that! Camping is supposed to be fun! Right?!

We're having fun, Right?!

July 20

Cabinet guy: "Here's where the fridge will be and here's where the island will be."

Me: "Ok."

Cabinet guy: "Let me draw it out for you." (draws picture on floor)

Me: "Ok."

Cabinet guy: (stands in space) "Here is how much room you will have."

Me: "OH!!!! Yeah, I'm a big girl. That's not much room. Lets move it."

Electric guy (By the way, his name is Ed, so I call him Electric Ed): mumbles....stammers....beats around the bush......and finally asks, "Are you a hot woman??!!" (LOL! meaning...do I have hot flashes?)

Me: "Yes! I am a hot woman."

Building a home is entertaining.

Week 5

July 24

There are three steps into the camper. I know that's not a lot, but its a camper. Campers are designed to hold a minimal amount of things. So, if you LIVE in a camper you have to find other places for all but the basic necessities. Therefore, you are constantly going in and out of the camper for stuff. And.....well.....the outhouse.

Three steps, 20 times, every day.

Every day is leg day, when you live in a camper.

July 26

Day......23?

My apologies to the people of Wal-Mart!

When camping, most of your time is spent outdoors in bright sunlight. Camper lighting is relaxing. It's soft, not bright. It's not for everyday living. Also, camping is considered an outdoor activity. Most of your time is spent outdoors in "the outdoors".

You will not find a full length mirror in a camper, or even a good mirror. The way you look isn't a priority.

Going to work, school, church or anywhere in public has now become a challenge. Unless you carry everything outside, you won't be wearing makeup. (One does NOT apply makeup in bad lighting. Sheesh! Every woman knows that, and if you don't know that, you will after trying it once.)

There is no room to style your hair and no mirror to see it in if you do. You can ask your sweet husband what the back of your hair looks like but will you really trust his answer?

When you live in a camper, ponytails go with everything... EVERYTHING!

And clothes you thought were clean enough to hang back in the closet...when you get to church and see them in good lighting...not so much.

When you see the people of Wal-Mart and are thinking: "Don't they look in the mirror before they leave the house?" (You know you say that.) Show a little grace. Maybe they live in a camper.

July 29 / Day 33

Living in a camper stinks! Literally.

You notice a camper stinks when you camp. You can't get away from it when it's where you LIVE.

You're gonna smell whatever you cook for dinner, until the next time you cook. When you open the door, that smell is the first thing to greet you. It gets in the closet, on your clothes, in your hair, and on your sheets and pillow. And if you...ahem...burn dinner, you're gonna smell that ALL NIGHT LONG.

Then there's the fridge. When you open the door, anything that has a smell in there is now in your house. You want to keep that sucker CLEAN. Throw out those leftovers!

But then, there's the trash. Same thing. The trash is in your living room, so anything that stinks in the trash also stinks in your living room.

Fighting camper stink is an ongoing battle. If I ever give up, you'll know. You'll want to stay more than six feet away from me. I burn a lot of dinners.

"Ok y'all! Cleaning the camper?"

You know how doing the house work takes all day? Spring cleaning? That was a whole week/month!

Camper cleaning is awesome! When you live in a camper, you can deep clean, spring clean, "Oh my gosh, my house has never been so clean!" in TWO hours! Honest! Top to bottom. Closets. Cabinets. Walls. Everything!

And if you're not overly dedicated to cleaning, you can take all day and also have a lot of camper naps.

When the husband gets home, he will say "Wow! This place is spotless! You must have worked so hard today!"

"Yes I did!"

Week 6

August 2 / Day ??

WOO!!! HOO!!! We are getting septic!!! Happy Day!

August 4

Sad day

The septic was put in, but we can't use it. The electric has to be hooked up to it, and there's no way to get the camper to it. So we keep using (and paying for) the porta potty.

August 5

Days? Weeks? Months?

This has more to do with building a new house than living in a camper, but we wouldn't be living in a camper, if we weren't building a new house. So technically, it's still a camper chronicle.

Maybe rethink the decision to do your own clean up. It's really hard work! You can't really do it at your own leisure. There are time constraints. For example: after the sheetrock guys are finished, all the scrap pieces have to be moved, so the next crew can get in. Construction guys are not neat. They just throw stuff everywhere. You gather it all into piles, then you load the piles on a trailer and take it all to a dumpster.

My husband works 40 to 50 hours a week at his job. My job is to manage everything going on here. I am making decisions, watching the money, paying the workers, and keeping day-to-day life going. I try to do all the cleanup that I can, so he doesn't have to spend all evening on it.

I'm loading sheetrock onto the trailer. There is a big stack right in the front door. (I'd like to point out here that it's right in the front door of what will soon be my new home.)

I pick up a larger piece of sheetrock and underneath it (where my fingers just were) is a copperhead snake all coiled up!

Of course, this is one of those times when there is not a soul here but me. My loud screams didn't alert even one neighbor, though I'm pretty sure they awakened the dead. I have become a pretty good jig dancer. I just know Riverdance are watching and considering recruiting me.

Now I have a dilemma. I don't want to let it out of my sight. I don't want it in my house. I don't want it in my camper. I don't want it in my barn. I don't want to step on it in my yard.

I can't go get the gun without losing sight of it.

"What to do?"

I decide to call the husband, even though I know he can't help me. I explain the situation. He says go get the gun. He is sure the snake won't move. There's no way he knows that, so I leave the phone there on a pallet of bricks. (Because he will hear the snake move and know where it goes?)

I come back with the gun and leave the phone on the bricks. I shoot the snake three times, scream like a girl the entire time, and then dance a nice jig.

When I pick up the phone, I hear laughter.

"Not funny, Husband!"

(But yes, he still laughs about it.)

He can laugh all he wants. I kept myself and my home safe today! I'm pretty proud of myself.

Week 7

If the camper's rockin'...

Whoever came up with that saying never spent much time in a camper. Campers are made to move, to take you from one place to another. They have to be flexible, so as not to come apart going down the highway.

They have no foundation. They are suspended in air.

They rock ALL THE. TIME!!

They rock when you come inside and when you go out. They rock when you shower.

They rock when you dry off after a shower.

They rock when you open doors looking for something.

They rock when the wind blows.

They rock when you're trying to get dressed in a tiny space.

They rock when you can't sleep and you toss and turn.

They rock when you walk from one end to the other.

When it's rainy, and I spend the day inside and then go out, it's like getting out of a boat after a long day on the water. You gotta get your "land legs".

If the campers rockin...come on in! But...yeah...you better knock first.

August 11 / Day 44

Things you can't have when you live in a camper:

Garden vegetables. Well, you can, but it's challenging. Remember, in the camper you have one room. Those gnats that you always get when you have fresh garden vegetables won't just be in your kitchen. You won't be able to get away from them.

Dirty dishes. (See previous entry about smells.)

More than one day of trash. (Also see previous entry about smells.)

Secrets

Privacy

Mystery in the marriage

Ten years. A minimum of ten years of marriage, before living in a camper. You better be certain of that love! You better have "until death do us part" locked down tight!

You're gonna know things. So many things. Things you

thought you wanted to know. Things you didn't want to know. Things you can't unknow. You're gonna know ALL the things.

"Why are you still in the bathroom? (Notice I didn't say outhouse.) You're shaving your legs... AGAIN?! How often do you have to do that? What is taking so long? What is that noise? You've been in there a long time. You have to put all that in your hair?"

All he needs to know is that you are beautiful. He doesn't need to know how you got that way, how long it took, how much it cost, or how often it's maintained.

But if you live in a camper there will be no more mystery. Only the toughest of marriages will survive.

August 13 / Day 46

If you're planning to live in your camper after you're fifty years old, plan to leave plenty of room in your freezer for icepacks. You WILL hurt your back...
Trying to shower in a teeny tiny space.
Trying to dry off in a teeny tiny space.
Trying to get dressed in a teeny tiny space.
Getting in and out of bed.
Making the bed.
Changing the sheets on the bed.
You're going to wiggle and squiggle and twist and turn.
You'll invent new yoga positions.
You WILL hurt your back. No, I'm NOT exaggerating.
You will hurt your back, no matter how old you are.
You're just gonna need icepacks, if you're over fifty.
Guaranteed.

And if you think you can keep it a secret from your husband...(see previous entry.)

August 14

Week seven y'all! Week seven!

I have to be honest, I never thought it would take this long. But on cleaning days, I love this camper bathroom! Makes me wonder... Do I really need two bathrooms? Do I really need a big bathroom? I can clean every inch of this camper bathroom, top to bottom, in fifteen minutes! What housewife doesn't love that? It's awesome!

And I don't clean the outhouse. Spencer from the porta potty service does that every Monday. You bet your sweet patootie I'm here to make sure there are no construction vehicles in his way when he gets here.

There are some good things about this camper life. It's all in the perspective.

Week 8

August 15

I've lost track. I don't know how many snakes we've seen and/or killed. We've been here 50 days, and I've seen...
Water snakes
Black snakes
Grass snakes
Ribbon snakes
Ringneck snakes
Copperheads

I'm not real thrilled that I can identify this many snakes.

I have, myself, killed one copperhead.

I stepped on a ribbon snake and had a close encounter with a grass snake.

I am in no way used to them. I don't like them. I want them all gone!

But.....I'm no longer terrified. I'm pretty ho-hum about it all.

I never ever thought I would say this, but I'm ready for winter. At least I won't have to constantly watch where

I'm stepping! Stupid snakes!!

August 18 / Day 1,762 (No? only day 53?)

PSA for anyone thinking of living in a camper, (or for the purpose of this particular entry, just camping) who is over fifty and clumsy:

I've had foot surgery. Rolling around on that little scooter isn't easy, or pleasant. Some things are just impossible, and everything is a hundred times more difficult. You do NOT want to be doing that in a camper. So if your only housing option is the camper, you're gonna have to be extremely careful.

You need to always be aware. ALWAYS!!

Also, we have a 5th wheel, which means steps on the inside. You must keep these steps in mind at all times.

The outside steps: Never carry anything up or down these steps. You WILL lose your balance, and it will be disastrous. Open the door and place all items on the floor, even your purse. Then, and only then, go up or down the steps. Do not experiment to see if I know what I'm talking about.

Steps that lead to and from the bedroom: They look innocent enough. There's two steps up from the main area, then about a three step hallway, with a door into the bathroom. Then there's another step up to the bed. There are no doors (except for the bathroom), so this is all basically one room just graduated in height.

In order to open the bathroom door, you have to step to the very edge of the first two steps with your toes hanging over the edge. If you have to go to the bathroom during the night (unless you have the outhouse option), it will be dark, and you will be sleepy, and you WILL step off the edge (not on purpose). It will be unpleasant, and you will no longer be sleepy. If you're over fifty, things could be broken. You do not want this. Do not conduct your own experiment to see if I'm right.

The step up into the bedroom is almost hidden by the bed. You wouldn't notice it, unless you knew it was there. If it's dark and you're sleepy, you WILL miss the step altogether, and this will not end well.

The hallway is not only short, but narrow. You can't even put your hands on your hips with your elbows out to your side. There's not a lot of room to fall. You will flail around in the hallway like a pinball in a pinball machine before landing on the floor. Trust me. No need to try your own experiment.

But night time is not the only danger. Concentrating on the many maneuvers to make the bed will cause you to miss the step by the bed.

Taking a camper nap or watching TV when someone suddenly knocks on the door will also be an adventure. You will forget the steps, but still have the added forward momentum of rushing to get the door. It's very possible to miss the first one entirely, stumble forward, not catch yourself in time, and tumble down the second set, at which time you will hit the linoleum and it's anyone's guess how you will land. Whether or not you're wearing socks will make a huge difference.

The only benefit of this scenario is... someone was knocking on the door, so you should be able to call for help. Providing you didn't lock the door, and it's not UPS or Amazon. They just knock and leave, never waiting for a feeble call for help.

Also, if you're in the bathroom and someone knocks, you will rush out the door, forget the steps, and a tumblin' you will go.

NEVER let the steps out of your mind. Camper life is dangerous.

Week 9

Picking out stain, paint, countertops, and flooring is exhausting. My brain hurts.

9 weeks

Nine. Weeks.

Nine
Weeks

9

weeks

August 24 / Week 8? 28? 42?

I was surprised by this camper fact. If you store food in plastic for a long time, it will smell like plastic. Not faintly. Very strong.

Everything goes in plastic in the camper, because otherwise, while you are boogying down the road, things will break.

That's just for camping for a week or two. When you're LIVING in the camper, you're gonna want to put it in glass or ceramic.

I put my staples in plastic containers. It's summer in Oklahoma! I'm not going to do any baking in the camper in the summertime. It's been eight weeks since I've used flour or sugar, but I can't eat my Wheaties without a little sugar sprinkled on top. (I don't want to hear your opinion. If I'm gonna eat grown up cereal, I'm gonna sprinkle a little sugar on it!)

I took the lid off and WHEW!!! Now the whole camper smells like plastic!

It tasted ok; I already had the milk poured; I wasn't gonna waste it.

If you're gonna live in the camper, put your stuff in glass containers.

You're welcome.

Week 10

August 29

View from camper window. Husband says the tree on far right looks like a dinosaur. He calls it the dinosaur tree. 😊

September 1 / Day 67

We've discussed the fall risks inside the camper and getting in and out of the camper. Now let's discuss the fall risks on a building site.

Before your house had it's nice porches and steps, you couldn't just walk into your home. It required a really big hike of the leg. For clumsy people (I think it's been established that would be me.), holding on to the door frame or maybe getting a helpful "butt" boost might be needed. Maybe an improvised step, like a five gallon bucket turned upside down in front of the door, will suffice. If you're clumsy, the bucket option is not a good choice. That sucker is not stable!

But sometimes you have to get in the house. Alas... Yesterday I had to go in the house, and I had an audience. It was one of the younger workers, who was maybe twenty years old. I stepped out of the house onto the bucket. It immediately tipped over. You've heard of your life passing through your mind? My future passed through mine. Broken bones, casts, surgery, knee scooters, etc.

In seconds, I quickly assessed HOW I wanted to fall. Should I catch myself with my hands and arms, thus having a broken arm, wrist, or shoulder? Or just fall? Broken ankle, foot, leg? Who knows.

I tried really hard to lesson the damage as much as possible. I bounced, hopped, jiggled, and flailed. I'm sure I made lots of unladylike noises. I would have made a great cartoon character at that moment!

Now for the young man. I was quite disappointed in that he never tried to help, never said a word, and never looked up from his phone. This all took place in the garage, so yes, he knew what was happening. But to be fair, I was bouncing like a pinball going for high score. He may have assessed the situation and decided that the only way to come out unharmed was to stay WAY out of the way. Or...I could be on some video streaming site.

Either way, all on my own, I avoided falling! (You may cheer! I know you were rooting for me.) It was definitely not done in a graceful manner, but all bones are intact. Nothing was harmed except my dignity. If I get through this with no broken bones, it will be a miracle.

Stay safe my clumsy friends!

September 2 / Day 68

Living on a building site should be its own chronicles, but for us they are intertwined.

Builders are worth every penny you pay them! They handle any problems that arise in the building of your home. Most of these problems you wouldn't even be aware of, if you didn't live on site. But if you DO live on site, you will be aware of (and sometimes responsible for) some of the day-to-day management.

Three A.M. Thunder. Lightening. Rain. Lot's of all three. I'm awake; the husband is not. (As previously mentioned, he will sleep through anything, except a gunshot. Zzz...zzzz...)

Did the trim carpenter put the windows down? Hopefully, but I don't know. I didn't go into the house, after everyone left.

Is the wind blowing enough for it to rain in? How much damage would it do?

How much damage would it do in an hour? The husband gets up for work in an hour. Then it would be his problem. (You're judging me now, but just wait.)

MY CABINETS!!!!!!! My brand new, custom-made cabinets are in front of the windows!

I'm wide awake now!

Guess who's going out in the storm?

I have a pair of imitation crocs that I've had for nine years. I slip them on when I need to go out quickly. They are orange and have flowers on them. My sister and I were at a garage sale, and she talked me into buying them. I tell you this, not because it has anything to do with the story, but because nine years later she still complains when I wear them. So every time I wear them or mention them, I make sure she knows they were her idea. My choice of footwear IS important to the story. Anyhoo... I slipped them on and headed out in my pajama's.

Camper steps are slippery when wet and even more so when wearing crocs. I slipped on the second step and missed the third one entirely. That should have been a furiously waving red flag! I made a swift recovery and started for the house.

Building sites do not have lawns or even grass. They have dirt, rocks, bricks, scrap pieces of everything, and equipment. Oklahoma has something called red clay. If you know what that is, you understand. If you don't, I can't explain it. That stuff has to be experienced! Plastic footwear is not a good choice for wet red clay. When I hit the clay, my feet looked like Fred Flintstone starting his car, and my arms looked like a bird taking flight. I managed to stay upright, but I have no idea how. I quickly realized that I wouldn't make it by walking across the building site. I was going to have to walk WAY around to find some grass. In the dark. In the rain. In my pajama's.

The day before, the builder had done dirt work to prepare for the concrete guys to pour porches, the driveway, and sidewalk. The entire house is surrounded by lots of nice, soft dirt, which is now lots and lots of mud.

How will I get into the house? I could go through the mud to the garage and use the bucket to get in. It has rained so hard that there is a HUGE puddle of water in front of the entire entrance. No way around. I have to go through. Another pile of dirt is directly in front of the garage entrance. I sunk up past my ankles. (Remember my footwear?) Now I have a pound of mud inside each shoe. Shoes that are plastic, wet, and now heavy. When I hit the garage floor, Fred Flintstone was back! I did catch myself in an extremely awkward position, just before I hit the concrete.

"Get up, shake it off, square your shoulders, and head for the bucket."

Thankfully, being drenched in rain has me wide awake. I approach the bucket like a 90-year-old woman getting in the shower. Fourth try and I am, relatively, safe inside the house.

I would have felt better about the whole thing if the windows had been up, and I had saved my cabinets, but everything was shut up tight. (Sigh...)

Now, back to the camper. I have to go back the way I came. It took a lot longer, and I got a lot wetter.

3:30 A.M. I'm showering and getting a pound of mud off my feet. Remember? There's no privacy?

"Honey? Are you showering?"

"No dear. You're having a dream. Go back to sleep."

September 4

10 weeks today.

Today

ten weeks today.

I'm ok. I'm ok. I'm ok. I'm ok. I'm ok. I'm ok. I'm ok...........

Week 11

No entries this week, but my husband caught a bucket full of sunshine one day, just for me. I'm so thankful he did, because now I can share it with you.

Week 12

September 12 / Day 78

Just sitting in my "yard" enjoying the view and the cooler temperature. I'm enjoying the nice evening and smelling the lovely aroma of my outhouse.

I have mentioned that we are building on ten UNIMPROVED acres. We are working on improving it. We have LOTS of trees. Beautiful trees! We are building on a little rise between two mature oak trees, so as to blend in with the landscape. We are further back from the road than is convenient, because we want the house to blend with the landscape. This place looks like a postcard! It's gorgeous!

The temperature has cooled and it is a perfect September evening. I'm sitting in my front yard in our lawn chairs, enjoying the breeze and the sun shining on the leaves. I see the sun sparkling on the pond in the distance. It's still a construction site, but the concrete and brick are finished. On the outside, it looks like a beautiful new house. Picture perfect.

Except for the smell. The picture is ruined if you look to the right. There sits the thing I love, and the thing I hate. My very own private porta potty.

Spencer is great! He's the guy that cleans my bathroom every Monday morning.

I try not to judge, but from the sound of the music that I can hear, which is literally a mile away, I'm pretty sure that Spencer is what is referred to as a metal head. And the way he looks seems to support that. I love Spencer! He is polite, kind, considerate, and helpful. He cleans my bathroom; he is here every Monday morning right on time. He cleans the bathroom, and he sprays some kind of deodorizer. A lot of it. I think he gives me more than the usual amount. The result of that is... you cannot smell what you think you would smell living within walking distance of a porta potty. And I SO appreciate that!!!! But...........after three months of smelling the deodorizer (I haven't been able to identify exactly what it smells like.), it is nauseating. I HATE that smell! OH! I hate that smell. But if you're outside, it's what you smell.

It's still September in Oklahoma, so it's hot most of the day. The tin box heats up quickly, but the A/C is a little much. You definitely don't want to open those windows. That's not something you want to breathe, while you're eating dinner. Leave the A/C on, and put on a sweater.

When you're outside enjoying the beauty, don't look to the right and try not to breathe too deeply.

September 15 / Day: a bazillion

Being sick in the camper sucks! And it doesn't matter if you're camping or living in the camper, it's a horrible experience either way.

Since there is only room for the necessities, there will be no stocked medicine cabinet with magical drugs to make all symptoms go away ...or at least better.

There won't be extra Kleenex available, so when you run out you have to use camper TP. Campers have to have special biodegradable TP, and that stuff is rough!

The bed is not comfortable. And when you go to the couch for a change of scenery, the camper couch is not comfortable. It feels more like a park bench than a couch. There's no walking from room to room looking out the windows.

There's no getting away from the husband so as not to contaminate him, thus ensuring that he can continue to go to work to pay for this glamorous lifestyle you are living.

And he can't get away from you while you cough, sneeze, snot, and hack. Yep, that "till death do you part" is starting to be a problem.

You better be sure of those "I Do's" before you think about living in a camper.

There's some ugly stuff goin' on in here.

September 16 / Day: a bazillion and one

Take your camper and set it on ten acres covered in ragweed and live in it. You'll find out if you have a ragweed allergy. But do it before you are on the backside of middle age. The older body does not respond well to this new condition.

Research will tell you that your body see's ragweed pollen as a danger and immediately begins war. War is for a younger generation. I do not have the strength or fortitude for this fight.

As mentioned before, I don't have the luxury of going to the medicine cabinet to choose a medication from my nice, on-hand supply. But never fear! In the fog of pain and sickness, I remembered that the medicine cabinet had indeed been "packed", and by packed I mean thrown in a box along with everything from the bathroom cabinet drawers and everything under the bathroom sink ...from both bathrooms.

I found the appropriate box and gleefully dumped the contents on the camper floor! Sweet medication!

NONE of it is the correct medication for this particular ailment, but I don't care. I will take anything to make this unholy misery go away! (Ragweed is an invention of Satan.)

FYI... If you have Ragweed allergy and take something to knock you out, when it wears off and you wake up, you will cough until you puke! Happy day!

Research also says to stay inside in air conditioning, even in the car. Fresh air is your enemy. It doesn't say what to do if you live in a camper on a construction site. (Even though the windows aren't open because of the smell, you still have to go in and out twenty times a day).

If I can get up the energy to make myself presentable, I'll head for the city today. Re-evaluate whether or not I have what it takes to be a country girl. I may be too old for this.

Hmmmm.........let's see what THIS medication will do.............

Camper Chronicles

Week 13

September 18

YEP!! You read that right. Twelve weeks (plus eight days). That's THREE months!

I haven't reached acceptance, and probably never will. This is not my home. It's the camper. It's where we stay when we need a break. It's where we stay when we're on vacation. It's a get-a-way. I've made it homey, but it's not home.

I love it! I'm so glad we have it. I'm thankful for it. But it's not home.

I have grown complacent. It is what it is. Challenging. Different. Some things are more difficult; some things are easier.

Being complacent has caused me to let down my guard. Remember the outhouse? The snakes? The dangers? The difficulties?

Remember how you always have to be mindful of the walk to the outhouse and the area around the outhouse? How you have to be aware of the INSIDE of the OUT-house?

If you never see a snake in these particular areas, after twelve weeks, you let down your guard. So imagine my surprise, when I grab the door handle and feel movement under my fingers?!!!!!

I'm pretty sure I am now completely qualified to be a member of Riverdance. (I expect them to call any day.) Anyone watching would have thought all my fingertips were on fire, but the exuberance with which I was shaking my hands would have only succeeded in causing my whole body to go up in flames. It was a sight to behold!!

Never fear! It was only a horsefly. But rest assured, I am back on high alert!

I no longer have to go to the outhouse, but I do need to do some laundry.

Happy Weekend friends!

September 21

This is true love.

It doesn't matter that she has five kids and an endless supply of laundry. Everything is ready for me to do laundry.

Best sister EVER!

September 22 / Day 88

I am a coffee drinker. I need the magic bean water to start the brain, to activate good behavior, to make nice words, and to activate the people skills. Being the delightful person I am does not come naturally.

Words you will probably never hear me say: "No thanks, I've had enough coffee."

Trying to time my morning trip to the outhouse between downpours... Yeah, I've had enough coffee. It's gonna be a bad attitude kind of day.

Of course, it's also trash day. The trash has to go half a mile (more or less), down to the end of the driveway. (We didn't consider that when we did all the planning.) It wasn't a big deal when the sun was shining, and I felt good about the extra cardio added to my making up the camper bed "workout". However, I'm not feeling so good about it this morning, without the proper amount of caffeination and having to walk through a monsoon.

Should I wear the imitation crocs......?

September 24 / Day 90

Ninety-eight days. That's a whole season. A whole summer! The. Whole. Summer.

Guess what I learned today? The hot water tank in a camper ain't very big.

(In case you have a puzzled look on your face, during summer in Oklahoma, in a tin box, you don't need a lot of hot water.)

I can either wash OR wash my hair. If I try to do both, one of them is gonna be in cold water. These great hair genes that gave me long, thick hair is usually a good thing. Not so much if you live in a camper.

If y'all see me at the Wal-Mart, don't be judgin'. I'll either be stinky or have nasty hair. You don't know where these people live. You better be showin' a little grace!

All y'all are so excited about fall weather. I'm gonna be prayin' for some Indian summer.

Week 14

September 25 / Day 91

The husband's doin' some improvin' on this unimproved mess. He's doin' a lot of clearin'.

I hear that diesel roarin', look out the camper window, and see him come over the hill like an Oklahoma tornado chaser! He throws open the door and says, "Git your shoes on!" Then he grabs the gun and says, "Come on!"

He had moved some brush with the backhoe, and a huge copperhead comes up outta there and heads for the next brush pile.

So..........he pulls the pickup next to the brush pile. I get in back with the shotgun. He gets on the backhoe. He's gonna pick up the brush pile, and I'm gonna shoot the snake.

I've always had the impression that ssssnnnaaakes are sssslllloooow. They are NOT!

That sucker came up outta there so fast, and it was the biggest one I've ever seen. It was coming straight UP out of the brush pile. I thought it was gonna jump in the bed of the pick up where I was standing!!

I froze for just a second.

Now I'm no stranger to guns, but I'm a loooooong way from being an expert. I had to shoot a fast-moving target, standing in the back of a pickup, while screaming and dancing the snake jig.

We don't have any close neighbors, and that's the only reason I'm not an internet sensation.

I got the snake on the first shot, but... I sure shot more than once.

Also, ...snakes keep moving after they are dead.

This is my life now.

September 27 / Day: I don't even know...........

YEE HAW!!! The camper is shakin' tonight! Anything that wasn't anchored down won't be here in the morning.

September 28 / Day: still don't know

My inspection for what the storm did last night is put on hold, along with a morning trip to the outhouse.

There's an injured coyote outside my window. Just hangin out, he's looking toward the camper occasionally. He's limping.

I'm going with my instincts on this one and staying inside. I can see what the wind blew away later.

September 30 / Day 96

Living in the camper in cold weather isn't the same as camping in cold weather.

There's no campfire, with marshmallows and hot cocoa.

It's just cold.

Week 15

October 2

There's not a lot of excitement anymore. (Well... except for snakes.) We've kind of settled into a routine, of sorts.

I'm still trying not to fall down the steps, and trying to stay off the construction site when it rains. Even the outhouse has become routine.

It's hard to remember what day it is. The days run together, we have no regular routine, and we're just getting through one day at a time.

Watching the house be built, or (because of the pandemic) just watching it sit, we're waiting on workers or supplies.

But summer has passed. Now it's fall.

Do you like fall? Do you like warm sweaters, cozy socks, flannel pajamas? How about waking up on a chilly morning and making a hot cup of coffee and snuggling under a soft warm blanket?

Yeah? Me too!

Well here's a little reality for ya'.

It ain't so great when all the sweaters, socks, pajamas and blankets are in boxes...in the barn. And even if you could remember which box, you probably can't find it. And if you can find it, you can't move the twenty boxes in front of it to get to it.

Campers don't have a lot of insulation. They get pretty chilly. Cold... It's cold in here y'all!!

I have to reevaluate my criticism of the summer people. They might live in a camper. I gotta learn to not be so judgy. Ya' never know why people are the way they are.

Now, if the husband reads this (and he will), and he says, "Just have one of those hot flashes." Then there will be a lot more excitement out here tonight. There's a backhoe here, and I might have to learn how to dig a deep hole.

Happy Fall Y'all!

October 5 / Day 101

Yes, you read that right. One hundred and one days. One hundred days, plus one day. There is no way to type that that makes it any less. It's still more than 100 days.

Again, with the rural unimproved land... When the weather turned cooler, all the woodland creatures said, "OH LOOK! The nice people have brought us winter shelter!"

They are all trying to find their way into my home ...or under it.

Last night the dog started growling at the floor. Once we determined that he hadn't just lost his mind, the husband took him outside, where he proceeded to go into serious "hunt" mode. Husband is now in pajamas with flashlight, encouraging dog.

Back and forth. Back and forth. "Where is it, Boy? Get it!"

After several minutes, Husband decides dog HAS lost his mind and tries to get dog to come in. "Come on! Let's go in!"

But dog refuses to come in.

And then...he finds it! The fight is on!

Dog yelps.

Now I'm worried.

I'm observing from the inside and can only see the husband in pajamas with flashlight...back and forth...back and forth...talking to the dog. ("He better not let the dog get hurt!")

At this point, I consider closing the front door, which he left open. A cornered animal just might run in.

"Get him!" "There he is!" "Get him!" "There ya go!!"

The next thing I know, Husband is holding up the biggest rat I've ever seen!

The dog is not an attack dog, only an alert dog. This displeases the husband, but I am grateful for the alert.

I hope this is not a nightly routine.

Also, the outhouse experience has become more challenging since having to keep a constant lookout for things that might have slithered in during the night seeking warmth.

This is my life now.

101 days.

Week 16

October 9

Camper beds.

The mattresses they put in campers are not made for sleeping on 106 nights in a row. You usually only camp a few weeks out of the year and not in a row.

If a camper mattress has to be replaced (and they are

never really meant to be), it has to fit out the camper door. So you see, you are not going to have a Sealy Posturepedic or a sleep number or a pillow top mattress.

When you sleep on it 106 nights in a row, you're gonna leave deep impressions. A slump. A hole. And you're not gonna get out of it.

If you can't sleep, and you're restless, you're not gonna be doing a lot of tossing and turning. It's like trying to roll uphill. If you have insomnia, this leads to a lot of frustration.

But it's ok. I also have a lot of anxiety. So this allows me plenty of time to worry about things I can't do anything about and things I can't change. It all works out.

Since the husband has to go to work everyday to pay for the new digs and needs a good nights sleep, I feel it's my duty to "fix" the mattress.

How to do this???

I will need to take a camper nap every day and sleep on the hump in between the two low places to even it out.

That's really the only solution.

I will make the sacrifice.

A sneaky snack and a camper nap every day.

It's a hard life but someone's gotta live it.

October 12 / Day 108

Be mindful of your breathing while in the outhouse.

If you choke on your own spit, you will have to cough.

If you have to cough, you will have to take a deep breath of outhouse air.

Then you will puke.

Stay safe camper friends.

Week 17

October 16 / Day 112

Stress and tensions are rising. That will happen with 112 days of close confinement.

This is gonna be long. Sit down and get comfy.

Insomnia... I'm not a fan of zombies. Don't read books about them. Don't watch shows or movies about them. But I'm pretty sure the walking dead are people with insomnia.

Regular life (the one with all the chaos) didn't get put on hold when we became the King and Queen of Camperville.

Nearing the end of construction. (PLEASE let it be so!) A lot more cleaning needs to be done. (My windows will never be this clean again!) More decisions need to be made...

If you love decorating, you've never built a new house. Good Grief! You have to decide what type and what color of EVERYTHING!!

Do you know how many different kinds of light bulbs there are? And so many different kinds of lighting!

Door knobs? Who knew there were so many options? And bathroom mirrors? Did you know your house won't pass inspection if you don't have bathroom mirrors?

Building loans, mortgages, paperwork, and every nickel being accounted for. Inspections. Decisions.

But I digress...stress and tensions. They are getting to me. I've had several meltdowns, but I try to make sure they happen when I'm alone.

Like the day my hands were sticky. I had reached a breaking point. My hands were sticky, and I couldn't find a source. I had washed my hands three times, and they kept getting sticky. I burst into tears, and even though I was alone, I said out loud, "WHY are my hands sticky?!"

Like a toddler, I needed some juice and a nap.

But I'm not gonna cry in front of the husband, so the meltdown he witnessed took the form of anger. (Also like a toddler.) Also over something sticky. (That must be my trigger.)

The floor. I had mopped it four times, and it was still

sticky. In the process of mopping the fourth time, I knocked over the sweeper. It came apart, and dirt went everywhere. The meltdown was building. I knew it was coming. I was trying so hard to hold it together. I tried to put the sweeper back together, for FIVE minutes. It would NOT go back together.

This was the point where an offer to help would have been good. That didn't come until several minutes later, and by then the volcano had already erupted. It just hadn't blown.

Had you been outside you would have heard the camper door bang violently against the side of the camper. You would have seen pieces of the sweeper flying out the door, as if they had been shot out of a rocket. Then, various other things went shooting out the door, like an NBA player trying to make a basket from half court. And then, the loud slamming of the door! After which, I took a shower and went to bed with no explanation. The floor is still sticky.

The husband thought it would be funny to tell this particular story to the Pastor. That tells me the stress and tensions are getting to him too, because he obviously didn't think that decision through. He can be thankful he's good-lookin'.

Stay tuned. There's a chance it will get worse before it gets better.

October 18 / Night time

Big Fat Liar!!!!

40 degrees outside

I come in from church and get in the shower. I know I won't have a lot of hot water, but it's still very warm. I decide I have enough time to put conditioner in my hair. The water is still warm. Not cooling off. Yay!

Maybe no bad hair day tomorrow! I close my eyes for one millisecond of bliss......and the frozen tundra pours from the shower head! No warning...no cooling off.....not even time to get out of the way!

I know the shower head did it on purpose. It lulled me into thinking I had more time.

Game on stupid shower! I will defeat you!

October 21 / Day 116? 117? 118?

I learned a lesson today. People really don't want to hear your platitudes. (I looked it up. That is the correct usage. In this case...VERY correct)

I've been guilty. When you don't know what to say you just pull out some overused saying, because....well....it has to be a good saying. Everyone says it. Right?

The conversation did not go as planned.

I was in a public place and saw someone I haven't seen in a long time. She asked how things were going, so I updated her, including the part about us becoming "camper people". She said, "I bet you've learned a lot from this experience."

I laughed and said "Oh yes! I've learned many things!"

Then she said " I imagine you've learned you don't need as much stuff."

I did mention how the conversation didn't go as planned?

My reply: "YES!! I need my stuff!"

"I want my stuff that I don't use very often, but when I need it, it's there."

"I want my stuff that I only use twice a year, but it's so handy to have."

"I want my stuff that is just to look at and has no other purpose."

"I want my stuff that I have to look for, because I can't remember which closet it's in."

"I want my stuff that's only purpose is.....it's different stuff."

"I want my holiday stuff to help me be festive."

"I miss my stuff."

"Can I get by with less stuff? Yes."

"Can I be happy with less stuff? Yes."

"But if I don't have to....then I want my stuff."

She was just being nice, saying what many others had

said. Poor woman. She may be traumatized. I should check on her.

Be careful what you say. Camper people can be testy.

Also, something in this camper stinks! It could be the bathmat. It needs to be burned.

I have another bathmat packed in a box, in the barn, somewhere....with all my stuff!

I really need my stuff.

Camper Chronicles

Week 18

October 25 / Day 121

Our camper days are coming to an end, but before they do, it only stands to reason (at least in my world), that they get more chaotic. But never fear! I reign supreme in the world of chaos!

We can't move into the new house yet, so we still live in the camper. But I can do laundry and shower in the new house.

We can't move anything in, but we can put "stuff" in the cabinets and closets. Everything else stays in the barn.

What that means is... we don't know where anything is.

I look for something in the camper; can't find it. Go over to the house; still can't find it. Out to the barn...not there. Then I realize it's probably in the camper, and I just didn't look hard enough, because I made a hasty assumption that it was somewhere else.

If you're a neighbor, you probably think I'm practicing to coach T-Ball. You've seen it. "Run here!!!" "No! ...Go back!" "No! Go on!!!" "Keep going!" "No! Go back!")

In fairness to me, it's deer season, and that stops for no one or nothing. So, we don't know where any of our belongings are. We LIVE in a camper, so all our everyday stuff is crammed into a space meant for a weeks worth of stuff. But we also have ALL our hunting gear in the camper. Hunting is a lifestyle all it's own and takes up a LOT of space, because it requires a LOT of stuff. My entire living area looks like a Cabela's rummage sale. The only clothes I can find are camo and hunter orange.

If you see me in Wal-Mart in camo and sandals and my hair not combed......judge all you want. I deserve it. But it won't change anything.

October 26 / Day 122

I warned you. I am the Queen of chaos, but I am married to the King, and we are good.

Practice makes perfect.

Yes, boys and girls, we have a leak! Woo Hoo!!

Temps are in the 30's, it's raining, and the northern gale is coming straight from the artic circle! "Saddle up and hold on tight!"

The husband is on the roof of the camper, trying to find and fix the leak.

The ladder has blown down twice.

As a side note, all of our winter clothes are in boxes in the barn. You bet I'm thankful for those hunting clothes right now!

October 27 / Day 123

We ran out of propane last night. For those that don't know....that's our heat source.

Remember... Temperatures are in the 30's, and the wind is coming straight from Santa's workshop.

And rain... (I saw a neighbor out with plans for Noah's Ark.)

ALL
NIGHT
LONG

The husband is awesome! (You know that.) Not one drop of water got in the camper. He is that good! Dry as a bone. I can't feel my fingers, toes or nose, but I'm dry!

Check on your camper friends in this weather. They are not ok.

October 28 / Day 124

Remember, we have inside toilets now? We still live on a construction site. I still have severe insomnia.

I go to the house to use the inside toilet, in my pajamas. Not the "these pajamas are so cute I will wear them to Wal-Mart" pajamas. These ones are the "I have insomnia, toss and turn all night, it's freezing cold!" pajamas - with hair to match. (Think...80's hair band on a weekend bender) and super dark insomnia circles under my eyes. (Pray for my husband. He gets to see that every morning.)

Also, remember, there are ALWAYS workers on a construction site.

Once you're "dried in" you have to leave a key accessible because apparently some workers will use not "having a key" as an excuse to leave and not work that day. But having a key means that even though the door is locked, they can come and go as they please.

So.......I come out of MY bathroom to find a strange man standing in the hallway. (Remember how I look?) Awkward!! For both of us! I'm pretty sure he wasn't expecting anyone to be inside (most people don't live on their construction site), and I KNOW he wasn't expecting the Bride of Frankenstein!

The trouble with an inside toilet is you get comfortable and forget it isn't your house quite yet.

He was the county inspector. I hope he passes us and doesn't think this has become a homeless camp.

Camper Chronicles

Week 19

November 2 / Day 129

18 weeks and 3 days have passed, since the day we moved into the camper. And now, it seems our time has come to an end.

Spencer is here. (The porta potty guy)

We had a tearful goodbye. It would be awesome if he could continue to be here every Monday morning and clean my bathrooms, but that is not to be.

I'll miss Spencer. But I am ecstatic to see the outhouse go! I was thankful to have it, but even more thankful for indoor plumbing!

We have moved out of the camper. I'm gonna be honest. There was a little bit of sadness, when we were emptying it out. But it didn't last long.

We stayed in the new house last night. OH! Good Gracious! This couch is SO comfortable! I haven't sat on real furniture for 129 days. I may have missed comfortable seating the most. On second thought, I probably missed indoor toilets the most. A comfortable place to sit, second. OH! A shower big enough to shave my legs! Enough hot water to shower AND wash my hair! Privacy! Room to pace! Closet space for ALL of my clothes! A washer and dryer! And my stuff!!!

It's everything we dreamed of! It was worth it! We are so happy!

But I'm going to miss you guys. I'm gonna miss sharing with you. I enjoyed making you laugh. It's been fun, but only because we took this trip together. Thank you for riding along.

Maybe I'll write a new chronicles. Maybe the challenges of starting a new life in our new home will warrant another journey that I can share with you. Moving to a new town, with a new lifestyle, in a brand spanking new house. (What could go wrong?)

Check on your camper Friends.

Don't judge those people at Wal-Mart...they might live in a camper.

Good bye for now...

***

Thank you for taking the time to read

<u>Camper Chronicles</u>

If you enjoyed it, please recommend it to others by taking a moment to review it where you obtained it.

You are welcome to visit the author's Facebook page at

<u>www.facebook.com/dottie.allen.1238</u>

Made in the USA
Columbia, SC
17 February 2022

55881771R00075